by Susannah Milham
illustrated by Peggy Tagel

HOUGHTON MIFFLIN BOSTON

Printed in China

ISBN-13: 978-0-547-01728-0
ISBN-10: 0-547-01728-6

3 4 5 6 7 8 9 0940 15 14 13 12 11 10

Look at Kevin and Lucy.
They liked to play together
all the time.

Kevin called Lucy
on the telephone.
"Can you come and
play with me?" said Kevin.
"I can!" said Lucy.

"Let's play this game,"
said Kevin.

"No!
I like to play with blocks,"
Lucy said.

"I want to play this game!"
said Kevin.
"But I want to play with
blocks!" Lucy said.

Kevin said, "Go home!
I don't want to play
with you!"

Lucy went home.
She was sad.
Kevin was her friend, and
Lucy did not like to
fight with him.

Kevin was sad, too.
Lucy was his friend, and
Kevin did not like to
fight with her.

Lucy called Kevin on the telephone.
"Can you come and play with me?" said Lucy.
"I can!" Kevin said.

Responding

TARGET SKILL Understanding Characters

Characters Kevin and Lucy are characters in this story. What do they say and do? What does this tell you about them? Make a chart.

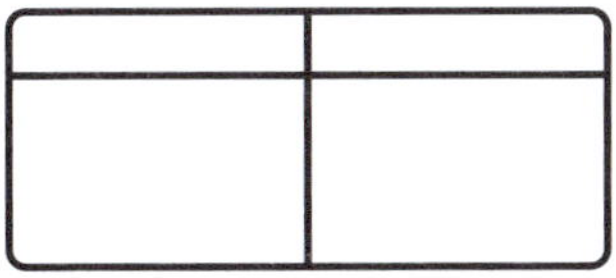

Write About It

Text to Self Make a list of things you like to do with your friends. Then draw a picture of you and a friend in a favorite activity.

make | play

LEARN MORE WORDS

fight | telephone

TARGET SKILL **Understanding Characters** Tell more about characters.

TARGET STRATEGY **Infer/Predict** Use clues to figure out more about story parts.

GENRE **Fiction** is a story that is made up.